THE
CHEAT'S
GUIDE TO
GOLF

THE
CHEAT'S
GUIDE TO
GOLF

COLIN BOWLES

HarperCollins*Publishers*

HarperCollins*Publishers*
77–85 Fulham Palace Road,
Hammersmith, London W6 8JB

This paperback edition 1994
3 5 7 9 8 6 4 2

Previously published in paperback by Fontana 1991
Reprinted once

First published in Great Britain by
Angus & Robertson (UK) 1989

ISBN 0 00 637786 6

Set in Century Old Style

Printed and bound in Great Britain by
Caledonian International Book Manufacturing Ltd, Glasgow

For Bryan, Dennis and Jock
who gave up a Sunday morning
to teach me the finer points
of this wonderful game

CONTENTS

"The only reason I ever played golf in the first place was so I could afford to hunt and fish."

SAM SNEAD

INTRODUCTION

It's not easy to be good at golf. It takes practice, luck, practice, talent, and more practice. The sad fact is, we can't all be Greg Norman.

And it's not cheap to buy yourself a round these days, either. In fact, some people say you should have as many shots as possible during your game to make sure you get your money's worth.

While this rationale might vaguely soothe your frazzled nerves when you've just finished a particularly appalling round, it doesn't help when you stand up to address the ball on the first tee. All you want to do is hit that ball straight, hard and out of sight.

The fundamental problem with golf is that every so often, no matter how lacking you may be in the essential virtues required of a steady player, the odds are that one day you *will* hit the ball straight, hard and out of sight. This is the essential frustration of this excruciating sport. For when you've done it once, you make the fundamental error of asking yourself why you can't do it all the time.

The answer to this question is simple: the first time was a fluke.

More often, the ball will only fly straight, hard and out of sight when you least expect it . . . such as when you are attempting a delicate pitch and run to the flag.

But don't despair. Even if you can't be good at the game, you can at least enjoy yourself every Saturday morning and *win*. The fundamental secret of enjoying golf lies not in playing well, but in taking everyone else's money—as in poker. In fact, think of golf as a way of playing poker without putting on weight and you're halfway to endless enjoyment. More specifically, it is possible to learn and adapt a number of ploys from that worthy card game to suit your ends on the golf course. What you are then playing is the highly skilled sport of Sly Golf—and that's what this book is all about.

Like any other sport, Sly Golf requires a certain amount of preparation and the right mental approach. Fortunately, however, it requires skills that are more easily acquired than the

1

extraordinary spatial awareness and hand–eye co-ordination of the professional golfer. The result is that no matter how badly you play your round, your playing partners will still end up feeling worse than you do.

So, no matter how bad a golfer you are, you can start winning *now*! All you need is a set of clubs, a bag, and a steely determination to crush and humiliate your friends.

Oh, and you'll also need *The Cheat's Guide to Golf*.

CHAPTER ONE

GOLF AND SLY GOLF

Although superficially similar in appearance (equipment, clothing, venue), golf and Sly Golf are actually worlds apart—as these vital definitions reveal . . .

GOLF

GOLF

An outdoor game for two or more players, each of whom uses specially designed clubs to propel a small hard ball over a field of play known as a golf course (see below). The object of the game is to advance the ball around the course using as few strokes as possible.

THE COURSE

The course is divided into 18 "holes". Each "hole" has at one end a starting point known as a tee (see below), and a small hole, or cup, in the ground at the other, marked by a flag. The ball must be propelled into the hole in order to complete the play at each "hole".

THE TEE

The players begin at the first tee, a level area of turf, usually raised slightly above the surrounding terrain. From here each player tries to drive the ball onto the fairway, or main part of the golf course, which is a carefully tended strip of land 30 to 90 metres wide, on which the grass has been cut to provide a good playing surface for the ball.

THE ROUGH

On either side of the fairway is the rough, which consists of areas of long grass, bushes or trees, sometimes containing sandy, rough

3

or marshy land, which compel golfers to use additional skills and judgment in playing their shots.

THE GREEN

At the far end of the fairway from the tee is the putting green, an area of closely cropped grass surrounding the hole or cup. The smooth surface is designed to facilitate the progress of the ball into the cup after the ball has been given a tap or gentle stroke known as a putt.

SLY GOLF

Outdoor conflict between two or more players, each of whom uses every means at their disposal to win money from their friends (enemies) while walking around a golf course (see below). The object of the game is to ruin the weekend for the others.

THE COURSE

The course is divided into 18 "holes". Each "hole" has at one end a starting point known as a tee (see below), at which the players gather to distract each other, and a small hole, or cup, in the ground at the other, marked by a flag. The ball must be propelled into the hole using the least number of strokes that can be proved by the other players.

THE TEE

The players begin at the first tee, a level area of turf, usually raised slightly above the surrounding terrain. From here each player tries to drive the ball into the rough (see below), where they will be hidden from view of the others.

THE ROUGH

On either side of the fairway is the rough, which consists of areas of long grass, bushes or trees, sometimes containing sandy, rough or marshy land a metre deep in golf balls which have been deliberately trodden underfoot, for reasons that will become apparent later. The rough compels Sly Golfers to use additional skills and judgment to avoid being caught cheating by the others.

THE GREEN

At the far end of the fairway from the tee is the putting green, an area of closely cropped grass surrounding the hole or cup, where most of the cheating and distracting takes place. The smooth surface is designed to facilitate the surreptitious progress of the Sly Golfer's marker closer to the hole while the other player is executing what is known as a putt.

CHAPTER TWO

THE HISTORY OF
SLY GOLF

The history of Sly Golf is, of course, inextricably entwined with the history of golf—and on many occasions the two games have been practically indistinguishable. Indeed, some historians have even gone so far as to conclude that the name "golf" is derived from the ancient Flemish word "kolfen", meaning "to cheat".

Golf as we know it today was devised by the Scots some time before the fourteenth century. And, human nature being what it is, Sly Golf developed soon thereafter. Its first high-profile occurrence, however, was in a game that took place in 1682, when James II, while a resident of Edinburgh, challenged two English noblemen to a game of golf to settle a dispute. He chose a humble shoemaker named John Pattersone as his partner. The nefarious details of the game are lost in the mists of time, but it *is* known that King and cobbler won . . . and that Pattersone was able to build a house in the town on the proceeds of the match. He is thought to have been the first champion Sly Golfer.

Then, just ten years later, a more momentous Sly Golf incident took place: a match between Scotland and England with side bets resulted in the Glencoe Massacre after a Campbell denied employing a Five Finger Wedge at the fourteenth.

It was all downhill from then on.

In the eighteenth century the first golf (and Sly Golf) associations were established; they included the Honourable Company of Edinburgh Golfers (1744) and the Dishonourable Company of Ex-Edinburgh Golfers (1745).

The first clubs established outside Britain were the Indian Thuggee and Assassins Golf Association (1829) and the US Renegade Apache and Riverboat Gamblers Club (1843).

At this time there was not the variety of clubs that are used in the contemporary game. Golf bags did not come into being until around the 1870s, which meant that "Ground Under Repair" signs,

transistor radios and other Sly Golf props had to be carried around under the arm.

The popularity of Sly Golf reached new heights in the 1920s and has steadily increased in recent years, fostered by television and the decline in public morals.

CHAPTER THREE

THE BASICS

(and the First Maxim of Sly Golf)

Let's face it. Unless you're winning lots of championships, golf can become a bit of a bore.

Just look at your fellow players. To them, golf is not a game, it is a neurosis. People who like golf are generally self-obsessed, egocentric, moody and obsessive about figures. Many enthusiasts are tax accountants, auditors, heads of organised crime, or politicians.

If you play golf as a form of relaxation, you are certifiably loony. True golfers do not play the game as a form of stress management. Quite the reverse. They play to establish superiority over (a) themselves, (b) inanimate objects such as a small white ball with dimples on it, and (c) their friends. All of which can become rather tedious.

Golf, like poker, just isn't interesting unless you're playing for money. There are a number of ways of doing this; one of the most popular—and most cut-throat—forms is known as "Skins".

Skins is played with four players. Each hole is worth a previously agreed sum of money. One player has to win the hole outright from the others in order to take the money and win the "skin". If there is no outright winner, the sum jackpots to the next hole.

So, say you're playing for $2 a hole: the winner of a hole will pick up $2 from each of the other three players. If there's no winner, the total $8 jackpots to the next hole.

As the stakes increase, so the game becomes more interesting. It can result in the sort of contest where American professional Fuzzy Zoehler won $150,000 on a single putt. The only thing that spoiled it for him was that the money was provided by a cigarette company and not Jack Nicklaus.

You may never play for such intimidating stakes yourself. But you can appreciate why golf is not a game to be treated solely as a sport.

OK, so winning isn't everything—but losing can be expensive. Which gives rise to the first maxim of Sly Golf:

THE END JUSTIFIES THE MEANS

CHAPTER FOUR

PREPARING FOR THE GAME

(and the Second Maxim of Sly Golf)

We will assume that you already know a little bit about driving, wedge shots, playing out of the rough, and putting. Good. Because that's the last we'll be saying about them. To be a great Sly Golfer requires skills of a different sort—in other words, those of cheating.

Fortunately, there's no need to feel in the least bit guilty about cheating at golf. That's because everybody cheats to some degree. It's part of the art of golf, the sheer poetry of the game. Golfers are very honest about this. Just look at the signs. You'll see them on every golf course: "PREFERRED LIES". Golf is the only game where lies are preferred to anything else.

But there is an art to cheating at golf, as at cheating at anything. To win by cheating alone is crass; the other players will think you won fair and square, and that can spoil the fun for the true exponent of Sly Golf.

The object is to win when all the other players *know* you cheated but can't prove it. Then, at the end of the day, you extract their money through the gaps in their gritted teeth.

No matter what the Bhagwan says, this is the road to true bliss.

PLAY TO WIN

Many golfers make the elementary mistake of trying to win by improving their game. This is unnecessary and often counterproductive. It distracts you from the main task at hand, which is to *disimprove* your opponent's game.

11

Many novices think that you win at golf by taking fewer strokes than your opponents. This is simply not true. You win at golf by making your opponents take *more* strokes.

There is a subtle difference.

Once you've got that clear in your mind, you must make certain practical preparations . . .

PRE-MATCH TACTICS

Any game of golf can be won the day before. There are a number of ways to do this, some more extreme than others.

Some of these methods are not guaranteed to make you the most popular member of the club. But if you're truly committed to winning—and what golfer isn't?—then you won't care.

First, you must know your opponents. If you're playing with your friends, you should already know their weaknesses. Exploit them ruthlessly. Friendship is fine, but it should never interfere with winning at golf.

To this end, it is always worthwhile having one of your opponents' (enemies') wives or girlfriends owe you a favour. Call in the debt by having her slip into her negligée and take her boyfriend/husband to bed for a long and passionate lovemaking session the night before the game. Make her promise to keep him at it until well after midnight and, preferably, once more just before he gets up to drive to the golf course.

This particular ruse has a devastating effect on most men's performance around the course the next day.

If you want to completely shatter his concentration, have her take *you* to bed for a long and passionate lovemaking session the night before the game. Then tell him about it just as he's about to tee off.

Women Sly Golfers should take advantage of coffee mornings at a friend's (enemy's) house by slipping into the main bedroom unnoticed (tell her you're going to use the bathroom) and stealing a pair of her husband's underpants. Then whip them out of your pocket on the first tee on the morning of the game, and say in an offhand manner: "Oh, Mary—these are Derek's. Will you give them back to him for me?" There is no need to elaborate.

Another distraction for Sly Golfers of either reproductive persuasion is to go round to a friend's (enemy's) house the night

before the game and let down a tyre on their car or dig up the front garden. Or both. It's very difficult for anyone to put in a good round if they've spent the first half hour of their day changing a tyre on their station wagon or gazing in cataleptic horror at the ruins of their prize rose bushes.

As with any sport, you should practise, practise, practise. No, not with the golf clubs, you dummy. You could stand on the driving range all year and improve your game only a couple of shots at best. What you need to improve are your Sly Golf skills.

Join a debating society or, even better, take up a career as a corporate lawyer. Learn the art of debate and pedantry. When you've reached the stage where you can argue articulately that the Pacific Ocean is casual water, then you're ready to begin.

Of course, if you're a *truly* dedicated Sly Golfer you'll also arrange for someone else to be at the golf course with you. No, not a caddy.

You may have to pay this person a small consideration, but it will be worth it. This person is known merely as your associate, and can be male or female, preferably both. More of this later.

Above all, always remember the second maxim of Sly Golf:

STOP AT NOTHING

CHAPTER FIVE

PROPS

(and the Third Maxim of Sly Golf)

Having scored some early points with your pre-match tactics, you are ready for the preliminaries at the golf course. At this stage, appearance is all.

You should start to aggravate the other players as soon as you meet them on the first tee. Show up with new gloves, wide check slacks, or the new Golden Bear clubs you borrowed from a friend, father-in-law or stroke victim three doors up. Anything that aspires to pretension on your part puts you a couple of points ahead before the first shot is played.

Vitally important is the brand-new, high-quality golf ball which you must unwrap from its box, screwing up the tissue paper, just as your opponent (enemy) lines up their first tee shot.

An American Express or Visa sticker on the side of your golf bag is another especially demoralising device.

SPECIAL EFFECTS

A devastatingly effective ploy, useful for club championship finals and skins games where the side bets are likely to be heavy, is to show up at the course wearing a black armband. Look morose.

On no account should you discuss *why* you are wearing a black armband. This should be left to your opponents' imaginations. Have a box of Kleenex in your golf bag and ostentatiously wipe away a tear occasionally.

Above all, keep a stiff upper lip. When the others press you about what is wrong, stoically repeat: "No, I'll tell you later. I don't want to spoil our game of golf."

You *will* spoil it, of course. That's the whole point.

EQUIPMENT

Equipment is not the most important part of a Sly Golfer's arsenal; a good exponent can win with a lacrosse stick and a putter stolen

from the local Crazy Golf course. However, there are some essential items that you should never reach the golf course without.

BALLS

All your balls should be the same number and the same brand.

If you start a par four hole with a DDH-4, for example, and reach the green with a number three Pinnacle and claim you're putting for an eagle, after a miraculous recovery from a wild hook into the rough, suspicions will be aroused.

Spare Balls Always have a very special spare ball with you, in case one of your opponents runs out. (People who play golf with Sly Golfers tend to lose more balls than usual.) Make sure this is clearly marked as your "spare" spare, because this is the one that you will have had soaking in a jam jar full of vinegar for the last two months, and then wrapped in a new, crisp wrapper.

The vinegar will have given it the consistency of a piece of pure granite, so that when hit with some force it will move approximately 6 metres while the percussion vibrates the user's spine like a tuning fork.

Don't forget to apologise and tell the poor bugger you gave it to that you'll take the ball straight back to the shop on Monday morning.

They won't believe you didn't do it deliberately. But they can't *prove* it. Another point to you.

CAHOOTS

Pro golfers have caddies. Sly Golfers have helpers known as "cahoots".

For male golfers, a cahoot is someone to whom you offer a free drink or a business favour in return for a small service on a Sunday morning. This service could take the form of driving past one of the tees next to the road at a critical moment and shouting: "Hit it with your dick, Baldy!" as one of your friends (enemies) is about to tee off.

A cahoot could also be a woman friend who, after some subtle emotional blackmail, you persuade to drive topless past the same tee and shout: "Hi there, boys!" as another of your friends (enemies) is taking a practice swing.

Women Sly Golfers should inveigle any of their husband's/boyfriend's less physically prepossessing mates to

17

stroll past the first tee in thongs, stubbies and Chesty Bond and yell out to one of your friends (enemies): "Hi, honey! Thanks for last night! Davo and Bluey enjoyed themselves, too! Don't forget to send us our change!"

If your companions are over 35, get one of your handsome young nephews to walk by at an appropriate moment and shout: "Hey grandma! Don't bend over so far! You're blocking the sun!"

Just make sure he doesn't yell it at *you*.

A cahoot need not necessarily offer only casual favours. A cahoot is also someone to whom you give $10 and an iridescent orange golf ball with your name scrawled on it in felt-tip pen. You then make an exact copy of this ball, possibly the only other one like it in existence.

Before your game, you arrange with the other players a substantial side bet if any of you scores a hole-in-one.

Then, when playing a hole where the pin is not clearly visible from the tee, or where you are playing into the sun, you deliberately overhit your shot so that it sails out of sight, secure in the knowledge that your cahoot has already placed an identical ball in the cup.

After the ball leaves your driver you shake your head and agree with the others that it's possibly a lost ball. The important thing to remember when you reach the green is NOT TO LOOK IN THE HOLE!

Search everywhere for your ball. Sooner or later one of the others will look in the hole—either through courtesy, routine, or in preparation for their putt—and they will see an iridescent orange ball with your name on it.

When told you have scored a hole-in-one, react with complete disbelief.

Of course, cahoot fees for this sort of stunt can be expensive, but it's worth it to see your friends' (enemies') faces. And of course, no matter what your cahoot charges, providing you've organised the bets well, you still make a handsome profit.

THE HIPFLASK

Always bring a hipflask of cold tea with you. The others will assume it's spirits, especially if you've already got a reputation as a terror on the nineteenth green.

Your opponents will usually react by allowing their concentration to slip. They will assume that your game will start

19

falling to pieces as the alcohol begins to take effect, and as you take more and more nips they will begin to get more and more worried.

They will usually mutter among themselves, preparing for the unsavoury task of having to carry you off the course or, worse still, having their membership revoked when you throw up over the thirteenth green.

The hipflask routine is a brutally effective distraction. And, that, after all, is what Sly Golf is all about.

Isn't it?

CLUBS

You should always carry some spare gear. If one of your friends (enemies) does not have a full set of clubs, you can offer to lend them one of yours.

Sticky Fingers You should have in your bag a club whose grip you have previously smeared with copious amounts of some sticky, pungent substance such as fish oil or a substance known among Sly Golfers as hiss—honey mixed with urine.

Having used the club once, your opponent (enemy) will find that their hands are tacky and uncomfortable, and every time they try to drive or putt, they are assailed by a faint but relentlessly unpleasant smell. It will be impossible for them to concentrate from then on.

Give Them the Shaft The *pièce de resistance*, however, is the club that you have pre-stressed by carefully sawing through the shaft and then re-gluing.

When used, the shaft will fracture immediately and the head will fly off into the bushes. Your friend (enemy) will be forced to apologise and tell you—truthfully—that they did not abuse it. You can smile ruefully and make a pretence of believing them. Stricken with guilt, they will ensure that you win the round in order to make amends. They may even buy you another club.

But don't count on it—remember the third maxim of Sly Golf:

NEVER TRUST ANOTHER GOLFER

CHAPTER SIX

ELEMENTARY GAMESMANSHIP

(and the Fourth Maxim of Sly Golf)

First, a word of advice.

Most people think they know what gamesmanship is all about, and assume that if someone is aware that their opponent is using gamesmanship, the effect is negated.

This is just not true.

Suppose you are employing a form of gamesmanship in your golf match, and the other players are all perfectly aware of what you're up to. It really doesn't help them to ignore you. It actually makes matters worse, because they start to concentrate on ignoring you, and forget about their own golf.

In fact, the power to irritate in minor ways is your most effective weapon. It can do to a good golfer's game what a family of termites will do to a balsawood dunny.

Only much faster.

Emotion is energy. Anger is a great deal of energy all wrapped up in a hard little ball. On the golf course this excess energy translates into belting the cover off the ball so that it overruns the green, or losing control of a backswing so that a nasty hook or slice develops.

To achieve this effect—known as the Psychopath Syndrome— amateurs often try to blatantly needle their opponents. This is a mistake. The image you should try to convey is one of genial conviviality. Remember the three keys to good golf, summed up in the fourth maxim of Sly Golf:

BE FRIENDLY, BE HELPFUL, BE CHEERFUL

After all, what are friends for?

21

BE FRIENDLY

When one of your opponents (enemies) fluffs their drive, you should chuckle and say something like: "Us old blokes can't hit the ball as far these days", or "Never mind, girls, we're not as young as we were".

To which, of course, the immediate knee-jerk response is: "You speak for yourself", muttered through firmly clenched teeth.

Any man under 70, and any woman under 130, deeply resents being categorised as "aged". After such a remark they will set their double chins in steely determination and attempt to belt the cover off their next shot. This is the time when slices and hooks make an unexpected appearance. Round one to you.

BE HELPFUL

Always be on hand to offer advice. Suppose one of your opponents (enemies) has hit their ball onto the fairway next to the lake. They are trying to make up their mind whether to play over the water hazard or waste a shot playing up the dogleg. This is your cue to pat them cheerfully on the back and whisper: "Forget it, you'll never make it."

They won't be able to help themselves.

They'll face up to the ball with a steely glint in their eye and try to hit it hard and high over the lake. Naturally, they will fail dismally. You just laugh and shake your head and say: "I told you so."

From that moment on they are doomed. No one can play a good round of golf when they are shaking with rage.

You, of course, remain innocent of any wrong-doing, frankly astonished that someone should blame you for luring them into playing a hopeless shot. "But Dennis/Mary, old buddy, I was the one who told you to play it safe."

What can they say?

Or, if someone is pulling to the left on their swing, commiserate with them. Mention it each time they step up to drive, and express the wish that the problem will disappear. Offer suggestions on how they might be able to correct the problem. In no time at all the minor flaw should be magnified into a major crisis of confidence that will infect all areas of the unfortunate victim's game.

BE CHEERFUL

Above all, retain your sense of humour. Especially when another of your friends (enemies) is attempting a difficult shot out of the rough around a huge white gum. Just as they've finished their warm-up swing, step up and whisper: "Hey, Al/Shirl, aim for the middle of the tree. If you do, you'll never hit it."

Then turn and join the other two in an explosion of harmless mirth. The player standing over the ball will straighten and glare at you for (a) breaking their concentration and (b) deriding their game.

You act abashed, blush in acknowledgment, and say: "Only joking."

The damage has, of course, been done. All you have to do now is stand well back so that you're out of the way when their ball rebounds from the trunk of that tree and whizzes past your ears at 200 kilometres an hour.

To summarise—always ensure that your opponents (enemies) are playing with a handicap: *you*!

CHAPTER SEVEN

ADVANCED GAMESMANSHIP

(and the Fifth Maxim of Sly Golf)

Elementary gamesmanship employs the relatively simple arts of irritation and distraction. Having mastered those skills, however, you must next learn the finer points of psychology (or, to be absolutely precise, psychological warfare).

You must avoid becoming distracted by mere golfing ability (either your own or others'), learn to turn your opponents' (enemies') strengths into weaknesses, and be prepared to change your tactics—to improvise—if necessary.

SERIOUS SITUATIONS

The classic means of turning opponents' strengths to your advantage is encapsulated in the fifth maxim of Sly Golf:

THERE IS NO SUCH THING AS A HARMLESS JOKE

"I hear the Queen's sending you a telegram when you break a hundred," is an example of a "harmless" joke.

The message is obvious: "Look, we're all a bunch of amateur misfits here, so let's stand back and laugh at ourselves."

But, of course, the simple truth is most golfers cannot laugh at themselves. They take the game deadly seriously. This is why Sly Golfers—who know they are hopeless—always win.

It is why shouting "Fore!" just as someone is about to putt is such a devastating tactic.

And always bear in mind that, for the same reason, smirking is a health hazard (for your opponents, of course). Thus, giggling can be a devastating addition to the Sly Golfer's armoury. After one of your friends (enemies) fluffs a shot, a simple "Oh, bad

25

26

luck, George/Mavis" said with a smirk is enough to drive a serious golfer insane.

ASPIRE TO THE DEPTHS

The greatest weapon Sly Golfers possess is their own self-image. They never aspire to anything greater than mediocrity. They are at all times self-deprecating, they never attempt difficult shots, and they are content to three-putt every single green.

Providing they win.

It is this motivation that raises them above mere mortals.

While those around them attempt to improve their game and lower their handicap, Sly Golfers are content to score a century every time they go out on the course.

Providing they win.

Unlike other golfers, they have no illusions about their prowess. They do not believe that they could have been a pro *if they'd had the time to practise*, which is the private credo of almost every other golfer.

Sly Golfers *know* they're hopeless. And that's OK.

As long as they win.

And, believe it or not, it's easy to win at golf—as long as you remember that this game requires *total* concentration. Too many players concentrate only when it's their turn to play. This is a fatal error. Great golfers are on top of their game the whole time they are on the course.

Once you begin to see the effects of some good pre-match tactics and a bit of well-executed gamesmanship, you may start to appreciate just how easy it can be to win at golf.

PUTTING YOUR GAME TOGETHER

However, let's assume that things are not going to plan.

The hook that you helped induce, by implying that the player was practically senile, has miraculously righted itself. Your pre-match tactics haven't worked either. The first guy's wife had a headache and the other guy really didn't give a damn about his rose bushes. He was going to put down brick paving anyway.

What now?

First—learn to play the big points, as tennis champions do. Keep your best moves for the big holes. Concentrate on maintaining consistency.

The good Sly Golfer's game is based on attrition. This is best done by keeping up an incessant level of chatter. Sex, religion and politics are the best subjects. Get two of your opponents involved in a heated debate over privatisation, Papal infallibility or Kathleen Turner/Tom Selleck and you're well on your way.

But there are three other areas of skill to look at: driving, approach shots and putting . . .

CHAPTER EIGHT

DRIVING

(and the Sixth Maxim of Sly Golf)

As every golfer knows, good timing is vital, especially on the tee. For example, you should know exactly the right moment in someone's backswing to turn on your pocket radio for the latest cricket score.

If a player has a poor technique, then it's pointless wasting energy trying to put them off their game. But if they're consistently putting their tee shot 200 metres down the middle of the fairway, stern measures are called for.

Remember—never allow a good player to tee off (especially on a par three) without telling the other two players a joke. The joke should be a short one, so that the player on the tee doesn't have to interrupt their swing to catch the punch line.

For example:

Q: What's the difference between having a hard-on and having the light on?

A: You can sleep with the light on.

Or, for the ladies:

Q: Why did God create man?

A: Because vibrators can't take out the garbage.

These are perfect gags for teeing off. First, and most important, they're in dubious taste. Second, they're short. Third, they involve sex. This combination usually erodes the concentration of even a hardened professional.

Another alternative is to inspect your ball as your main opposition lines up their shot. Comment on an "onion" cut (imagined), or dimple, and tell everyone loudly that you are replacing it. Have a brand new specimen on hand, make sure you are upwind, and then "accidentally" drop the tissue wrapping so that it *just* flashes in the corner of their eye on the downswing.

BRONCHIAL UPSWING

Bronchial upswing is the name given to a sort of cough caused by the sudden congestion of the bronchial tubes brought on by an opponent's perfect swing.

Just as your opponent (enemy) brings the club back over their shoulder for their shot, you cough. Just once. Timing is vital here; the cough should be executed just as the player is moving into their downswing and it is too late to abort the shot.

This is a tactic designed to win rounds rather than individual holes. It is more akin to trench warfare than the hydrogen bomb. You employ Bronchial Upswing for three consecutive holes, until your opponent is starting to become a little irritated.

Then on the fourth hole you say something like: "I promise not to cough this time." Of course, they don't believe you. As they go into their downswing they are waiting for you to cough.

You don't.

On the next hole you cough. On the next hole you don't cough. On the hole after that you say you won't cough, and do. The next hole you take a deep breath and put your hand over your mouth on their upswing, as if you're about to cough—but you don't.

The effect of all this is quite shattering. Unless they have the concentration of a chess master, by the time the player is halfway through the round they are thinking more about your cough than they are about golf.

You've achieved your goal.

You've ruined someone else's Sunday.

THE MAGNET EFFECT

Another useful technique is the Magnet Effect. This is based on Bowles' First Law of Dynamics, which states:

Any round object must travel in a straight line directly toward any obstacle which the player is trying to avoid.

Let's see how this works.

Your opponent (enemy) has placed their ball on the third tee and is about to drive. It is a nice wide fairway, but there is a shallow lake about 50 metres to the right. It's supposed to form

an obstacle on the sixteenth. Hundreds of golfers play this course every week and none of them have ever put their ball in the lake from the third tee.

All you have to say is this: "Stay away from that lake over on the right-hand side, George/Mavis." That should do it. It is now aerodynamically impossible for George/Mavis not to slice their ball into the lake.

What is even better is that they'll realise it was your fault and they'll silently resent you for the rest of the round. No one can play good golf when they're seething. Remember Bowles' Second Law of Dynamics:

The number of strokes required to complete a round will increase in direct proportion to the player's diminution of self-control.

H O W   D O   Y O U   D O   I T ?

Didn't fall for it, huh? They laughed about the shot going in the lake and played their next shot next to the pin for a birdie putt? What do you do with people like that?

Here's what.

You ask for advice. You look mournful and confess that your own game seems to be going to pieces. "You're driving so well, George/Mavis. How do you do it?" This question has to be said with complete sincerity and you should then wait for an answer.

Ask them to display their own drive for you, in slow motion, while you watch and try to pick up pointers.

"Do you inhale or exhale when you drive, George/Mavis?" Wait while they try to answer that one. They probably haven't got a clue. If you've got a good swing, you don't have to think about it. And that's the key.

When they've thought about it a while and made up their mind that they exhale—they think—wait for their next drive and then say: "Gee, George/Mavis, you're finishing with your right elbow really high and then your left ankle just seems to pivot a little while your right hip sort of sashays out in the opposite direction as you exhale. Is that the secret?"

Now you know what will happen from here. First they'll start asking themselves what they're doing right and then they'll try to exaggerate it for your benefit when they drive. Once they've started analysing themselves they're gone.

32

Occasionally one of your foursome will drop out and someone will invite a friend along to make up the number. This person will turn out to be amiable, charming, and—damn their eyes—a good golfer. This is an intolerable situation and no Sly Golfer should allow it to continue.

Your initial gambit should be to say, innocently, just after one of their drives: "Have you played a lot of lacrosse?" That's all. You don't have to elaborate. Until the next tee.

This is when you say: "Where did you learn that grip?"

The natural reaction will be something like: "What's wrong with it?"

You simply shrug and say nothing. This alone will guarantee their next drive will hook or slice.

At this point you step in and offer advice. When offering advice there are three areas of driving you should draw attention to:

THE GRIP

The grip Sly Golfers always teach is the Penis Grip. This is when you tell a player that they are holding the shaft too tightly. "Relax. You should hold it gently, caress it." Then *sotto voce:* "Like it's your own/your husband's penis."

It can then be very instructive, not to say entertaining, to stand back and watch while your opponent (enemy) attempts to follow these instructions. If you're squeamish, don't look.

THE STANCE

The Sly Golfer always teaches the Rodin Stance: "You keep your eyes on your left knee while your right shoulder draws back parallel with the jawline, keeping the left shoulder tight to the chest as if you're trying to hold a plover's egg underneath, then swing your hips to forty-five degrees, with your left ankle pointing back to a point midway between your right foot and an imaginary line drawn between your other knee and your golf bag."

THE SWING

The Sly Golfer passes on useful tips like the Bruce Lee Swing. With the Bruce Lee Swing you release your pent-up energy in a sudden verbal explosion, something between a snort and a scream. If you can actually persuade one of your group that this

THE RODIN STANCE

might be a useful part of their game, not only will you add 10 shots to their scorecard but you will also have the other players completely unnerved.

SIDE BETS

If one of your opponents is playing really well, they may be willing to contract for side bets. This is your opportunity to:

1. Win some money back, and
2. Erode their game.

There is a cardinal rule involved here, and it forms the sixth maxim of Sly Golf:

NEVER EVER BET ON YOUR OWN SKILL

Betting on your own skill is courting disaster. You should only ever wager on your opponents' lack of it. "Bet you can't clear that lake with your driver", or "Bet you can't land it on the green from here"—that sort of thing.

If they're playing well, they'll take the bet, with predictable results. After they've lost the money they took from you by skinning the last two holes, they'll start to get annoyed with themselves.

Just as you're about to play safe up the fairway, they'll probably come back at you with something like: "Bet you can't clear the dogleg from here." That's your cue to laugh good-naturedly and say, "Now, now, you can't put that old chestnut over on me", and when you refuse to bite they'll get even madder.

That's *their* golf ruined for the day.

EMERGENCY PROCEDURE

OK, you've got a really tough case. Their ball ended up in the lake and they just laughed it off. They refuse to coach you. Instead they offered to take you aside after the game at $50 an hour. (This is what *you* should do if anyone tries it on you.) Worse, they refuse to take side bets.

Don't worry. All is not lost.

Your final alternative is to whip out your virile member and invite the other two players to admire it. Make sure there's plenty of money riding on the shot, as this is an extraordinarily effective ploy and is almost guaranteed to win you any hole.

However, this ploy can be used only once.

Unless you are exceptionally vain.

If you're a woman, you can suddenly begin to describe, in lurid terms, the time you made love to a basketball team in the back of your Honda. Use plenty of hand movements; photographs, too, if possible.

All's fair in love and golf.

CHAPTER NINE

APPROACH SHOTS
(and the Seventh Maxim of Sly Golf)

No competent Sly Golfer should ever find themselves in the position of being uncompetitive by the time they get to the green.

Getting to within putting distance of the hole is not what Sly Golf is about. It is a formality and should be treated as such. A nice relaxing walk before the real battle is joined.

PLAYING INTO THE ROUGH

On no account should you ever lose a ball and incur penalty shots. Not ever.

In fact, one of the skills of Sly Golf is to aim for the deep rough and play from there. Like many guerilla fighters before you, you'll find that the protection and disguise of the jungle are your best friend.

This is where spare balls, all of the same make and number, come into their own. When your ball disappears into the rough, march off and tell the others: "You play through. I'll see if I can find it."

You then get far enough away from the others to be out of their vision. Find a good lie, with a clear shot through to the green. This is the spot to put one of your spare balls.

Don't draw attention to yourself by shouting: "It's OK, I've found it! Gee, that was lucky!" This invites suspicion. Simply take your club out of your bag and play through with as little fuss as possible.

If you do find your ball, ignore it unless it has a good lie. Tread on it, if it's too conspicuous. If someone else claims to have found your ball for you, simply deny it. Pick it up as a "find", then walk on another 50 metres and slip your spare down your trousers onto a good lie.

THE GROSBY WEDGE SHOT

If your ball is in a terrible lie, you can employ the Grosby Wedge Shot. Soccer players can improve their golf game out of sight—so to speak—by employing the casual flick of the toe.

THE FIVE FINGER DRIVE

If you're completely out of sight of the others, you can save yourself a lot of time and trouble by employing the Five Finger Drive.

This is done by positioning yourself over the ball, ensuring your back is straight, and looking up once to make sure no one is looking. You then pick up the ball and throw it as far as you can in the direction of the green. Cricketers and baseballers will find this particularly suited to their talents.

PLAYING FROM THE ROUGH

If, God forbid, you actually have to play your ball out of the rough with one of those funny-shaped things in your bag called a golf club, it would be wise to first take some precautions.

The rules of golf require you to try and play your way around all manner of strange objects. For example, if there is a newspaper or cigarette packet in the way of your ball, you are allowed to remove it, as such things are classed as "artificial obstructions".

However, you are not allowed to remove "loose impediments" such as dead rats or mice. Therefore you should always have a spare newspaper in your bag, so that if a dead rodent is obstructing your ball, you simply slide the newspaper underneath it. You can then remove the newspaper and the carrion at the same time. Simple.

So always have a copy of the morning paper on hand. However, for things like a dead cow, you may need Saturday's classified advertisements.

If your ball has landed in thick bush, stern measures are called for. Don't forget you are allowed to take practice swings. Good,

PLAY THE GAME FOR KICKS

DON'T THROW THE GAME, THROW THE BALL

firm practice swings over a half-hour period can clear an area of about half a hectare of all loose grass, branches and small saplings.

Remember to test the direction of the wind. Throw any small trees or iron stakes in the air and see which way the wind takes them.

PLAYING FROM THE SAND-TRAP

A variation of the Five Finger Drive is the Five Finger Chip Shot, which is by far the easiest way of playing out of a sand-trap.

Hold the club in your right hand, and hit the sand to give the right percussive effect. Then throw the ball out with your left hand. Instead of throwing overarm, you throw underarm, à la Trevor Chappell. Always remember to throw up a handful of sand with the ball.

We can't have anyone accuse you of cheating.

For this reason remember to never ever allow an opposing player to play from a bunker without standing and watching them. Even better, stand in the bunker with them. Breathe down their neck, if they'll let you. Just as the club strikes the ball, you intone: "That's one."

This alone should cause the ball to remain in the sand-trap. From then on, things can only get better—for you.

Count each shot aloud. After three or four attempts you can start to miscount. As they play the fourth shot you yell "Five!" Not only will the ball stay in the sand-trap but the player will turn purple and scream at you that that was only their fourth shot.

All right, so they've already lost the hole, but an experience like this can ruin the rest of their round.

And that's the whole object of the game.

Well, from your point of view, anyway.

HOW DO YOU LIKE YOUR STAKE?

Always keep a supply of white stakes in your golf bag. The rule book states: "A ball lying within two club lengths of a staked tree must be lifted and dropped clear."

41

CLEARING LOOSE IMPEDIMENTS

With a little practice, the technique of removing a stake from your bag and placing it clandestinely into the ground next to the tree where your ball has landed can be easily mastered.

THE GOLDEN ACANTHUS RULE

The Golden Acanthus Rule states that: "A ball lying within two club lengths of a staked tree must be lifted and dropped clear except when the tree does not lie between the ball and the green and except when the tree is a Golden Acanthus."

The Golden Acanthus Rule cannot be found in any official rule book. The Golden Acanthus Rule is also a model for any rule which you make up on the spur of the moment, and which you don't mean to enforce.

What happens is this. You see one of your friends (enemies) pick up their ball and drop it clear of a staked tree. You then state the Golden Acanthus Rule to them. They will naturally object and protest that they have never heard of any such rule. You shrug and say, "Oh, all right, I suppose it's only a game. But by rights you ought to be penalised a stroke. But never mind." Then walk away.

The object of the Golden Acanthus Rule is (a) to make the other player testy and irritable, and (b) to place them psychologically in your debt. You have caught them out in an infraction of the rules and have been prepared to be magnanimous.

This ensures that they will be less inclined to be pedantic about the rule book if they later find you removing branches with a chainsaw.

FIND IT AND GRIND IT

Remember—always volunteer to help your opponent look for their ball. If you find it, tread on it firmly, covering it with loose dirt and leaves if possible. Then stick close to your friend (enemy) to ensure that they don't try to use their spare ball and pretend it's their real one.

Some people will stoop to anything.

43

When searching for a friend's ball, always remember the seventh maxim of Sly Golf:

FIND IT AND GRIND IT

Not only is this an extremely expedient move, it also offers an incredible thrill comparable to parasailing or rogering your best friend's wife/husband.

CHAPTER TEN

PUTTING

(and the Eighth and Ninth Maxims of Sly Golf)

It's not until you're on the green that the game really begins. It's where the money's won and lost. If you've been paying attention up to now you should be on the green safely, and in a position to win the hole. At the very least, you must be able to stop anyone else winning.

It's time to get serious. Hard cash is involved. Remember the eighth maxim of Sly Golf:

DRIVE FOR SHOW, PUTT FOR DOUGH

By this stage one of the others will have blown out in the woods, the sand, the water, or all three. So your chance of winning will be at least 3 to 1. A good Sly Golfer can reduce these odds dramatically in their favour. Like 50 to 1 on.

HOW TO SCORE

However, you should be prepared. It is possible that the friends (enemies) you're playing with are . . . well, cheats. Now it hurts me to say this but some people have a fairly lax interpretation of the gentlemanly rules of this game.

So never tell the others how many strokes it took you to reach the green. (Of course, *never* say a whack, two throws and a kick.) To the enquiry "How many?" your response should be "What's yours?".

In golf you should always answer a question with another question. It is absolutely imperative that you discover first how many strokes *they* are claiming.

What you do then is simply deduct one stroke from the best score of your three playing partners—even if you have to stretch the laws of improbability past the law of gravity and through the theory of relativity.

I once stood on the green of a par five, 40 minutes after each player had stepped off the tee. Every player had spent at least half an hour of that time either in the woods or the sand-trap and I'd seen three balls land in the lake.

But by the time we actually reached the green each player was playing for a birdie putt and the one whose first two drives had landed in the water hazard had a one-metre tap-in for an eagle. This is what makes golf such a wonderful game.

THE LIE

Retaining your air of good-natured bonhomie, discuss the green in detail with the remaining players. Criticise the surface. Exaggerate breaks out of all proportion.

You should offer advice and encouragement to each of your three opponents (enemies) in turn. Sow the seeds of doubt. Tell one player: "The green looks a bit fast." They won't believe you, of course, but you'll get them thinking about it.

Now wander over to the second player and murmur thoughtfully: "There's a bit of a break to the left, isn't there?" They won't believe you either, but chances are that they'll overcompensate and then have to watch their ball roll away to the right.

Now go to the player whose ball is closest to the pin and tell him that the hole's as good as theirs. "Lose this and you've only got yourself to blame."

That really puts the pressure on.

A useful hint: lie about the state of the green only once. For the rest of the game you should tell the absolute truth. Everyone will assume you're lying and will begin to doubt the evidence of their own eyes.

PUTTING

The same rules apply to the green as to the tee. Timing is vital.

Never allow a player to step up for a crucial putt without saying something. You might, for example, comment on their putting style to one of the others. (In a whisper just loud enough for them to hear, of course.) "Gee, she's got a great stance, hasn't she?"

Or turn to one of the other players and say: "Don't worry, he's a choker. He'll three-putt this." No player likes to be known as a choker.

It makes them choke.

Just as the player is about to play the putt is the time to observe: "Now remember—hit it nice and firm."

HELP THE OTHER PLAYERS

After a while some players may make the outrageous claim that you're distracting them. Don't argue. Make an all-out effort to become invisible.

The next time they step up to putt, stand slightly off to the side so that you're just within their peripheral vision. Take a deep breath and stand stock still with your hands at your side, to attention. Quiver a little.

If the player asks what you're doing, keep your eyes fixed on a distant point and say: "My lips are sealed. I don't want to distract you."

You will be chagrined to learn that your tactics may cause other players to lose some of their rhythm on the green. You should commiserate and try to be of assistance.

Give them some free coaching. Stand behind them and offer: "I think it's your grip." Just that. Nothing else. Let them think *that* over for three or four holes.

Then, after the effect of that has worn off, offer some more advice. As with your earlier advice on driving, your comments should be irrelevant, gratuitous, personal and distracting.

This is the time to bring in the coaching about the other player's grip that we talked about earlier.

Stand behind them as they're about to make their putt and say: "Hold the putter lightly. Fondle it. Like it's a lover."

Used on the right player, this ploy can have devastating results. An impressionable player with a strong imagination can have their game ruined for the rest of the day, and in some cases for the rest of their life. If Marjorie's thinking about being in bed with Richard Gere, she's not going to make that 2 metre putt for the money.

And if Darryl's thinking about Dolly Parton every time he picks up his putter, his whole game's going to be a bust.

So to speak.

THE STEVE DAVIS TAP-IN

Another useful ploy. If you have an easy tap-in to make, especially fairly early in the round, play it this way: lie face down, reverse the club in your hand and tap the ball into the hole as if you were playing snooker. Almost certainly one of the other players will object and claim the shot is illegal. Just smile and walk off to the next tee, saying something like: "Come on, fellas, it's only a friendly game."

Leave the issue of the one illegal shot unresolved. If one of the other players gets upset about it, it will play on their mind for the rest of the round. Refuse to be drawn into argument about this. After all, *you* don't want to be put off your game as well.

That would defeat the object of playing that shot in the first place.

There's one important point to remember here: don't play the Steve Davis Tap-in if you're a bust at snooker. Play a shot like that and *miss* and the rest of the players won't let you forget it.

You'll have snookered yourself.

LOOK OUT FOR THE WIND

Be versatile. If one ploy doesn't work, always be prepared to try another. For example, if one of your opponents looks like they have a winning putt, you should start a discussion about their mother's imagined sexual habits.

It doesn't hurt, either, to mention the sum of money the player might win if the putt is a successful one. "Concentrate, Harry—don't forget this one's worth twenty bucks." This is usually enough to save the hole.

Flatulence can be another useful weapon. With correct usage, a healthy blast at the crucial moment has been known to put a semi-professional with a one-metre tap-in back in the sand-traps.

A doner kebab for breakfast with a glass of warm Foster's should see you through 36 holes and a sudden-death play-off. A tin of baked beans and a pint of Guinness would get you through the British Open.

MARKING THE BALL

Never ever let your own concentration lapse.

For example, you should always be able to gain an advantage when marking your ball. Putting down the marker, picking up your ball, picking up the marker, replacing the ball ... that's a lot of hand movements—and should gain even the most inexperienced golfer another metre at least. More if you're at the back of the green.

Where possible, use a magnetic marker and nonchalantly move it nearer the hole with your putter when no one is looking.

PULLING THE PIN

Another handy tip: always volunteer to hold the flag for the other players. As they're about to putt, you frown and mutter: "Watch out for the break to the left." They will usually stop their shot and glare at you.

Smile and say: "Sorry, just ignore me."

I've yet to see anyone sink a putt after I've done this.

Holding the pin is also your insurance policy. If someone is about to unexpectedly pull off a 20 metre putt from the back of the green you can be a little tardy in removing the pin and knock the ball backwards with the stick.

Not only will you save the hole but you will have ruined your opponent's golf for the rest of the day, if not the year.

Remember to apologise.

NEVER GIVE UP

The hallmarks of a true champion are determination and persistence. They never quit and they never know when they're beaten. This is also true of the dedicated Sly Golfer.

THE RUB OF THE GREEN

When you and an opponent have tap-ins about the same distance from the hole, your opponent might be tempted to shrug and say: "Play a gimme?" It is important never to answer this question. What you do is shrug. This can be interpreted as agreement, and if so, it works to your advantage.

But the moment they pick up the ball and start to walk off the green, say, "Wait a minute—what are you doing?" Then call a foul and claim the hole.

If it's raining, you can offer to hold an umbrella over your friend (enemy) to keep the worst of the wet off. Then, after they've sunk the winning putt, penalise them under rule 9-1(b) of the Royal and Ancient, which says: "A player shall not seek or accept physical assistance or protection from the elements."

DARE TO BE GREAT

Remember—never concede a putt. Never ever. Make them play it. Any situation can be saved, with a little imagination.

One Sly Golfer saved a 60 centimetre tap-in for $200 by vomiting over his opponent's (enemy's) ball. Keep plenty of syrup of ipecac in your bag. It's this sort of dedication and commitment that earmarks the truly great golfer.

And never ever forget the ninth maxim of Sly Golf:

NO ONE EVER GOT TO BE GREAT BY PLAYING IT STRAIGHT

CHAPTER ELEVEN

GENERAL TIPS

(and the Tenth Maxim of Sly Golf)

Never be a poor sport. A Sly Golfer is cheerful, helpful and in good humour at all times.

Don't ever appear upset that you're losing.

If someone else is playing well, tell them about it. Express the hope that they can keep it up for the whole game. Enquire about their best round ever and suggest that if they can be consistent and not lose their rhythm like so many other players do, they might be able to lower their handicap. Suggest ways they can eradicate flaws in their putting.

When their game starts to fall to bits, as it inevitably will, express sympathy.

Remind them it's only a game.

Tell them that even Greg Norman chokes.

On the other hand, when you get on top—as you undoubtedly will if you practise hard at the skills we've discussed in this book—never let the others forget it.

If you save a hole with a flukey 15 metre putt when one of the others has a half-metre tap-in for the money, it should become your only topic of conversation for the rest of the day.

Invite the others to do better. "Put another one up close and make it a challenge for me."

Or, "That was a great second shot of yours. Right next to the pin. If it had gone in, you would have won the hole."

When you win a hole, don't be gracious. Inform everyone you take American Express and Visa Card if they can't afford to pay cash. No cheques, please.

The final tip is the tenth maxim of Sly Golf:

WHEN YOU TAKE THE NOTES, REMEMBER TO GLOAT

CHECKLIST

What every Sly Golfer should have in or on their golf bag:

New golf ball in crinkly fresh tissue paper (to unwrap while one of your friends (enemies) is tee-ing off)

American Express or Visa symbol

Black armband (to elicit feelings of sympathy/morbidity)

New box of Kleenex (for loud blowing of nose on putting green)

Umbrella (for enforcing R&A rule 9–1(b))

Large number of spare balls, all identical

Pre-stressed club (for loan only)

Club with odiferous handle and vinegar-soaked golf ball (both clearly marked; for loan only)

Iridescent ball with your name written on in felt-tip pen (for hole-in-one)

Hipflask of cold tea (for feigning drunkenness)

Packet of potato chips and pocket radio (for use on tees and greens in emergencies)

Joke book (for distractions)

Chainsaw (for playing out of the rough)

White stakes (for playing around trees)

Artificial obstruction, such as a newspaper (for removing loose impediments)

Tin of baked beans and bottle of Guinness (for creating flatulence)

Magnetic markers (for advantageous putting)

Golf clubs (optional)

GLOSSARY

away
Far enough away to be out of sight.

carry
Put the ball in your pocket and carry it closer to the fairway.

casual water
Water.

chip
Chip away at another player's concentration.

choke
Something you pretend to do just as your opponent is about to tee off.

green
Someone who believes you really did hit a hole-in-one.

grip
What players lose in the presence of a truly great Sly Golfer.

lie
Anything said on a golf course.

lip
What you give to other players to put them off their game.

pitch and run
What you do when helping someone look for their ball in the rough. You pitch it in the lake and then run away.

rough
What you say to the player whose birdie putt you have just knocked off the green by "accidentally" removing the pin too late.

scratch
What you do when someone steps up to putt.

CHAPTER TWELVE

PSYCHOLOGICAL PROFILES

To be a truly great Sly Golfer you don't need to know much about golf, but you do need to know a lot about people. Sly Golf is psychological warfare in pleasant surroundings.

All golfers fall into separate, distinct categories. Once you know the personality, you can figure out ways to destroy it. That's what friends are for.

Especially in Sly Golf.

The following guide should help you attain some of these vital people skills.

MOUNT RUSHMORE

Silent and Serious. These types are solid, dependable golfers with great powers of concentration. Hard to draw into conversation. Usually remain aloof from heckling.

Best way to handle is to make fun of them. Cannot endure this. Once they get really upset, apologise and leave them alone. Although slow to anger, they usually require 24 hours to calm down.

THE GREAT WHITE SCHMUCK

These types show up at the course with brand-new Golden Bear golf clubs—not to try and put the other players off their game but *because they genuinely believe they are better than the rest of you*, despite previous evidence to the contrary.

After three holes disillusionment sets in and they're ready to throw their Golden Bear clubs in the lake. The art of handling this type is to keep their frustration at the maximum pitch without drawing the string too tight. Maintain the rage. You want to take the poor slob's money, you don't want them suicidal.

MOUNT RUSHMORE

THE GREAT WHITE SCHMUCK

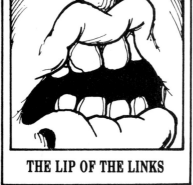

THE LIP OF THE LINKS

POCKET TREVINO

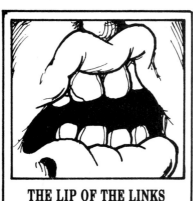

DELUDED BY GRANDEUR

THE ICE MAN

THE LIP OF THE LINKS

Erratic golfers. Their main problem is they can't keep their mouth shut. They only play golf to get a captive audience for their gossip, jokes and opinions for a couple of hours. They are a great boon to the Sly Golfer, as they put all the other players off their game. Wear earplugs.

POCKET TREVINO

Your friendly golf-course clown. They don't take anything seriously. Never a threat as golfers as they're only there for fun. Idiots.

Treat them like a Lip of the Links and tune them out.

DELUDED BY GRANDEUR

Amateurs who think they *could* have been a professional if it wasn't for their husbands/wives/children/second mortgage on the dishwasher/BMW with the sunroof holding them back and if only they'd taken up the game when they were younger. Eighty per cent of all amateur golfers fall into this category.

When they miss a shot, say things like: "Never mind, we can't all be Greg Norman/Jan Stephenson." You'll hit a raw nerve every time.

THE ICE MAN COMETH

Immune to gamesmanship. Refuses side bets. Laughs off any heckling.

The only way to deal with this type is to ask for advice. Their benevolent, easy-going nature is their weak link. They'll stop thinking about their game and try to help you. They don't realise until too late that their own game has gone to pieces.

HOW GREEN IS MY ROOKIE

A talented novice, usually a future national amateur champion on the way up.

Easy prey while still at the social stage; like shark round an effluent pipe, they'll swallow absolutely anything. Teach them the Rodin Stance and the Penis Grip and ruin their Sunday. Perhaps even ruin their career if you're lucky.

THE HECKLER

This type has no finesse. They antagonise everyone. Take some of your own medicine and don't rise to the bait.

Hecklers can dish it out, but they can't take it. When they miss a shot, that's the time to give them heaps. They'll fall to bits. The heckler is really just a disillusioned Great White Schmuck.

HARRY HAEMORRHOID

Oscar the Grouch in plus-fours. Reacts violently to the good-natured ribbing that is the Sly Golfer's stock in trade. It even improves their game.

Best way to handle them is invite a Pocket Trevino along for the game. If none available, get them talking about how the country is going downhill and how taxes are crippling business. Get them moaning about the government and they'll take their frustrations out on the ball.

The female version is Deirdre Dreadful. Start her talking about how the world is full of ungrateful daughters and good-for-nothing sons-in-law and she's finished.

NICE GUYS DOUBLE-BOGEY
(or, the female version)
THE THATCHER IN THE ROUGH

This type is the true competitor. Like you, they play to win; but they do it because of a deep psychological need, rather than your own innocent pleasure in humiliating and fleecing your friends.

The best way to put them off their game is to patronise them. After they've sliced their drive or missed a one-metre tap-in, say: "Oh, bad luck. Win some, lose some", or "You can't win 'em all". This self-evident truth is totally alien to their philosophy, and constant repetition of it will have them doubled over after nine holes with their peptic ulcer inflamed.

THE CHEAT

The worst possible kind of golfing partner. You can't trust them out of your sight for a moment, and they'll try all manner of gamesmanship to try and put you off your game. Despicable.

THE ROOKIE

THE HECKLER

HARRY HAEMORRHOID

DEIRDRE DREADFUL

NICE GUYS DOUBLE-BOGEY

THE CHEAT

61

CHAPTER THIRTEEN

A TYPICAL GAME OF SLY GOLF

The players:

BRYAN: One of the world's great Sly Golfers.

MO: A ten handicapper, deluded by grandeur.

RALPH: All style, no substance. In short, a Great White Schmuck.

GRAHAM: A social player. Plays just for the fun of it. In short, a simpleton.

Bryan parks his Rolls Royce in the car park. As he gets out, a small boy approaches and says:

"Mister, do you want me to clean your car while you're playing? Only five bucks."

Bryan, being a good-hearted fellow (off the course), says Sure and then goes off to the first tee to find his three partners for the day.

He arranges a side bet with Mo: he bets him that he can't go round the course with the same ball. Mo is delighted to take Bryan's money. If he plays it safe all day he may lose every hole, but will be compensated by Bryan's $100 at the end of it.

They head off to the first tee . . .

THE FIRST HOLE

Ralph steps up to the tee and drives. His shot flies high, straight and long, lands on the green, rolls towards the flag and rolls into the cup. A hole-in-one.

Bryan applauds and steps on to the tee.

"Right," he shouts, "the rest of us will have our practice shots and then we'll start, shall we?"

THE SECOND HOLE

Ralph, Mo and Graham are waiting on the green. They are all putting for par fives. Bryan has been gone some time. His tee shot landed in the trees at the side of the fairway, and occasionally they hear shouted oaths and see bits of twigs and leaves flying onto the fairway.

Finally, half an hour later, they see the ball hurtle out of the nearby trees, bounce onto the green and roll to within centimetres of the hole. Graham, feeling a surge of pity for a fellow golfer, gives the ball a gentle nudge with his foot to roll it into the hole.

When Bryan finally appears on the green, flushed and sweating, he looks around at the others and puffs: "Where did it go?"

"It's in the hole," Graham answers, straight-faced.

Bryan stares at him in disbelief. He goes to the hole and peers in, astonished. Then he straightens up, beaming: "Fantastic! I got an eagle!"

THE THIRD HOLE

Bryan slices his tee shot into the rough. When he reaches the green he applies the Sly Golfer's Rule of Diminishing Returns— he divides his actual score by two and claims three shots.

"But I heard you take six," Mo complains.

"The rest were to kill snakes," Bryan answers.

Meanwhile Ralph is putting for a birdie and the hole.

As he's about to putt, Bryan says to him: "Gee, Ralph, your wife's great in bed."

Ralph double-bogeys.

The other two take five shots and Bryan again takes the hole and is $12 richer.

"Gee, Bryan," Graham says as they are walking onto the next tee, "poor old Ralph's really upset. Why did you say that about his wife being good in bed?"

"Yes, I know. I shouldn't have," Bryan admits. "She's a rotten lay really. But I didn't want to hurt his feelings."

THE FOURTH HOLE

Bryan is in trouble. By the time he reaches the green he has committed the unpardonable sin of being uncompetitive. The others are putting for par, but having sliced two shots into the water from the tee, Bryan can reasonably claim only five, even after spending half an hour in the rough.

As he steps onto the green, he stops suddenly. "Look at that!"

He bends down. "This could be dog shit," he says.

He reaches down, picks it up. "Looks like dog shit."

He raises it to his nose. "Smells like dog shit."

He licks it. "Tastes like dog shit."

He throws it into the scrub. "Gee, that's lucky. I nearly trod in that."

The other three players look green. Bryan takes the hole by one shot and is $18 richer.

THE FIFTH HOLE

Ralph is having trouble with his swing. He is getting more and more angry as the game progresses. He attempts to correct his slice by sheer force. His first two swings are air shots.

"Not playing my normal game today," Ralph mutters.

"Oh?" Bryan says. "What game do you usually play?"

Ralph grits his teeth and swings again. Misses.

"Your swing's improving," Bryan offers. "You're missing much closer than you used to."

Ralph's face reddens. Another almighty swing. Another almighty miss.

"Difficult course, this one," Bryan sympathises.

Ralph smashes his driver on the ground.

THE SIXTH HOLE

Ralph is having a tough time. He's in the rough and tries to play a five wood between the trees. The shot rebounds off an old eucalypt and nearly decapitates him.

"Wrong club," Bryan tells him. "I would have used a nine iron over the trees for that."

Ralph's next attempt is a nine iron over the trees. It goes too far and lands next to the lake.

"Wrong club," Bryan mutters. "You should have used a seven iron."

Ralph looks across the lake to the green, 150 metres away, and then looks at Bryan.

"Well," he says, between gritted teeth, "what club would you use for this one?"

"Doesn't really matter," Bryan answers. "Just use a very old ball."

THE SEVENTH HOLE

Poor Ralph. He's in the rough again. He tries to play a nine iron out—straight into a sand-trap.

"Wrong club," Bryan tells him. "I would have used the five wood."

Ralph plays out of the sand-trap with his wedge. Right into the trees on the other side of the green.

"Wrong club," Bryan tells him. "I would have used a nine iron."

Ralph takes out his eight iron and smashes it against the trunk of a nearby tree.

"No, no," Bryan moans, "you should have used your five iron for that."

THE EIGHTH HOLE

By now, Ralph's game has deteriorated beyond all recognition. His first two tee shots land straight in the water. Bryan, seeing the opportunity to rub salt into the wound, offers to give him a little free coaching.

"You're holding the club too tight," he tells Ralph. "Hold it gently and lovingly. Pretend it's your own penis."

Ralph does as he's told. Bryan's ploy misfires because Ralph's next drive goes 200 metres straight up the middle of the fairway.

"How was that?" Ralph asks.

"Great," Bryan tells him. "But next time take it out of your mouth."

THE NINTH HOLE

Bryan's scheming has backfired. Ralph is feeling decidedly cocky by the time he reaches the short par-three ninth. "Just a drive and a putt for this one," he grins and shapes up for his tee shot.

His drive travels all of 10 metres.

Bryan gets down on all fours behind the ball and looks towards the green. Then he goes to Ralph's golf bag and hands him his putter.

"Remember," he says in a stage whisper, "hit this one nice and firm."

THE TENTH HOLE

The tenth hole is a dogleg par four. Mo and Ralph have gone on nature walks and scored quadruple bogeys. Bryan has a 10 metre putt for a five. However, Graham's approach shot has faded beautifully to hang just 5 centimetres from the hole. The gimme gives him a par four and the money, which has jackpotted to $40 for the hole.

"You don't want me to hole that, do you?" he asks cheerfully.

Bryan shakes his head. "No."

Graham grins, pockets the ball, and holds his hand out for the money.

"Now, wait a minute," Bryan says. "You didn't win that. You didn't putt out."

Graham stares at him, aghast. "But you said you didn't want me to!"

"Of course I didn't want you to," Bryan replies. "It would have cost me ten bucks if you had. All square. See if you can do better on the eleventh."

THE ELEVENTH HOLE

Bryan reaches the green safely and they are all putting to share the hole. Just as Mo is about to putt, Bryan shouts, "Wait!" and points to the road beside the course. A funeral cortege is passing by. Bryan removes his cap and lowers his head until the hearse has passed.

"Gee, Bryan," Mo says, "that was a nice gesture."

"Yes, I suppose it was," Bryan tells him, "but I was married to her for twenty-three years and I felt it was the least I could do."

THE TWELFTH HOLE

The twelfth is a par-three dogleg. One side of the course disappears into a deep ravine.

Ralph and Mo play conservative shots that fall short of the dogleg, but Bryan overhits and his ball disappears into the valley.

He re-emerges half an hour later to the green, where the others are waiting for him.

"How many shots?" Mo asks.

"Three," Bryan says. "Same as you guys."

"Wait a minute," Mo says. "The valley magnifies the noise. I heard six shots."

"Three were echoes," Bryan smiles, and putts through to win the hole.

THE THIRTEENTH HOLE

Mo has sliced his tee shot and it has landed in the rough. Like a good Sly Golfer, Bryan has gone with him to help him find his ball. Unfortunately, Mo gets to it first. It is lying in long grass but within clear sight of the green between two tall trees.

Mo examines the shot critically.

"I saw Greg Norman play this exact shot on this same course a couple of years ago," Bryan offers. "He used a seven iron."

Mo says thanks, gets out his seven iron and drives towards the green. The ball falls short and lands in a deep sand-trap.

"Should have used my nine iron," Mo grumbles.

"Yeah," Bryan agrees, "that's what Greg Norman said."

THE FOURTEENTH HOLE

The fourteenth is a short par three. Before they tee off, the three agree on a side bet of $100 if any one of them can get a hole-in-one.

Bryan and Mo both land short, but Ralph's drive lands right on the green, bounces three more times and drops into the hole.

Ralph is ecstatic. After a brief dance of celebration he holds his hand out for the money. Bryan hands over $25.

Ralph is not pleased. "But we agreed on a hundred!"

"For a hole-in-*one*," Bryan reminds him. "Your ball bounced four times before it went in!"

THE FIFTEENTH HOLE

Bryan is determined to get his money back. But his first tee shot lands in the water. His second lands in the rough.

"Give me one throw," he says to Ralph, "and I bet you fifty dollars I can still win this hole."

"You're on," Ralph agrees.

Mo reaches the green in six, Bryan in five. But Ralph is on in three and putts to a few centimetres from the pin.

"Aren't you going to use your throw?" he asks Bryan.

"Sure am," Bryan tells him, picks up Ralph's ball and hurls it into the bushes 100 metres away.

"But . . ." Ralph stutters. "But . . ."

"You agreed to one throw," Bryan tells him, "but I didn't say I was going to throw *my* ball."

He takes the hole and the money.

THE SIXTEENTH HOLE

The sixteenth hole runs parallel to the freeway. As Graham shapes up for his tee shot, he slices his drive and the ball bounces across the highway. A motor cyclist runs over it and crashes sprawling off his bike. A lorry swerves to avoid him and crashes into a bus. Bus and truck roll over, exploding into a raging inferno. More cars pile into the smouldering wreckage. Seventeen people are killed and 48 injured.

Graham holds his head in his hands. "What am I going to do?" he moans. "What am I going to do?"

"Well, if I were you," Bryan tells him, "I'd alter your grip just slightly like this . . ."

THE SEVENTEENTH HOLE

Mo has been losing steadily all day, primarily because he has been concentrating steadfastly on not losing his ball. Now he is on the seventeenth green, still with the same ball he started with.

"One hole to go," he says to Bryan with a grin. "Better get your money out."

"Not yet," Bryan answers. He picks up Mo's ball and hurls it into the lake. "You owe me a hundred dollars."

THE EIGHTEENTH HOLE

Ralph has not won a hole all day. He is desperate. Finally, on the eighteenth, he has a 30 centimetre putt that will win him the hole and a paltry $6—he has already lost $34.

As he shapes up for the putt, Bryan whispers: "Now try and keep it low."

He overhits the putt.

Ralph picks up his putter and snaps it over his knee. He drags his golf cart down to the nearest water hazard and tips it in. He throws his shoes in after it.

He goes in to the club bar, tells everyone they're all wankers and they can stick their lousy game up their fundamental orifices. Then he picks up an ashtray and throws it at the picture of Jack Nicklaus hanging on the wall.

He marches up to the locker room, grabs a towel from his locker and ties one end around a high grilled window in the lavatory and the other end round his neck. He climbs up on the toilet seat and prepares to hang himself.

On his way past, Bryan sticks his head in the door. "Feel like a game next weekend, Ralph?" he shouts.

Ralph unknots the towel and jumps down from the lavatory seat. "What time?"

Bryan, $100 richer, not including another $125 won on side bets, makes his way back to his Rolls Royce in the car park. The small boy who has been cleaning his car is waiting for him.

"Great job," Bryan tells him. "Here's your money."

"Thanks," the boy says. "By the way, when I was cleaning the inside of the car, I found these. What are they?"

He holds up a pair of golf tees.

"They're called tees," Bryan tells him. "You put your balls on those before you drive off."

"Jeez," the boy says. "Rolls Royce think of everything, don't they?"

CHAPTER FOURTEEN

QUIZ: DO YOU HAVE WHAT IT TAKES?

Think you've mastered the techniques of great Sly Golf? Well, here's your chance to prove it. Consider the following your graduation examination.

Answer each question as clearly and concisely as possible. Extra points will be awarded for cheating.

1. What is a good lie?
(a) Finding your ball on the middle of the fairway with a clear shot to the green.
(b) Finding your ball in the rough, but on a slightly raised mound with no impediments around it, and with a clear shot through to the green.
(c) Taking 40 minutes to get onto the green of a par four and telling everyone you're putting for an eagle.

2. One of your playing partners has sliced their drive from the tee into the lake. What should you say?
(a) Nothing.
(b) "Oh, bad luck."
(c) "Oh, bad luck," and snigger.
(d) Roar with laughter.

3. Your best friend has recently lost his job and just last week his wife left him. He's joined you for a game of golf to take his mind off things. He's just taken 15 shots on a par three. What should you say?
(a) "It's only a game."
(b) "Good thing it's only match play."
(c) "Happens to the best of us."
(d) "Lost your job, lost your wife. Can't you do anything right?"

4. One of your playing partners is about to attempt a one-metre putt for a $48 skin. What should you do?
(a) Keep quite still and say nothing. (That's good etiquette.)
(b) Keep quite still and fart. (That's good tactics.)
(c) Keep quite still and shout "Fore!" (That's a good joke.)
(d) Fart, shout "Fore!" and turn on the radio. (That's what they'd do if it was you.)

5. Who is your personal hero?

(a) Greg Norman (a) Jan Stephenson
(b) Seve Ballesteros (b) Hollis Stacey
(c) Tom Watson (c) Nancy Lopez
(d) Ronald Biggs (d) Lucretia Borgia

6. One of your playing partners has hit their tee shot into the rough. They go off to look for it. You volunteer to help them. You find it in a perfect lie, with a clear shot between the trees to the green. Do you:
(a) Shout: "It's all right. I've found it!"?
(b) Nudge it into a depression with your toe and shout: "It's all right. I've found it!"?
(c) Ram it down the neck of an empty Coke bottle, replace it and shout: "It's all right. I've found it!"?
(d) Stamp on it with your foot and say nothing?

7. Your own ball has landed in the rough. You find it at the bottom of a disused sand quarry in the middle of a forest of lantana, where it has become wedged between two large rocks, which appears to be the ancestral home of a large tiger snake. Should you:
(a) Try and play out of it with your seven iron?
(b) Call the snake an artificial obstruction, move the ball two club lengths away and play a nine iron?
(c) Take a stroke and distance penalty?
(d) Hit the snake with your sand wedge and play a Five Finger Drive with your spare ball?

8. The Club President has just seen you employ the Five Finger Wedge out of a bunker. What do you do?
(a) Confess to your playing partners immediately and forfeit the hole.

(b) Resign from the club immediately.

(c) Take the Club President aside and offer him a bribe.

(d) Take the Club President aside and threaten to employ the Grosby Wedge Shot into his generative organs if he says a word.

9. **The wife of one of your friends has too many drinks at a party and confides to you in strictest confidence about an affair she had three years ago. Her husband has never found out. What should you do?**

(a) Keep it to yourself. After all, he's a friend.

(b) Just tell your wife. You have no secrets from each other.

(c) Leave cryptic notes in your friend's golf bag.

(d) Wait till he steps up for a $64 putt and say: "Hey, Gra', guess what I heard the other day . . ."

10. **Your ball has landed next to a "Ground Under Repair" sign. How far are you allowed to move your ball?**

(a) Two club lengths.

(b) Two boat lengths.

(c) Two kilometres.

(d) To wherever you want.

ANSWERS

1. (a) 0 (b) 0 (c) 2
2. (a) -2 (b) 0 (c) 1 (d) 2
3. (a) and (c) 1 (if said with the right degree of sarcasm) (b) 0 (d) 2
4. (a) -2 (b) 1 (c) 2 (d) 5
5. (a) 0 (b) 0 (c) 0 (d) 2
6. (a) -2 (b) 1 (c) 2 (d) 3
7. (a) -2 (b) 1 (c) 0 (d) 2
8. (a) 0 (b) -2 (c) 1 (d) 2
9. (a) 0 (b) 0 (c) 1 (d) 2
10. (a) 0 (b) 1 (c) 2 (d) 5

HOW DID YOU SCORE?

OVER 15

Congratulations! You have qualified as a Sly Golfer. The world of fame and fortune awaits. Well, notoriety and fortune, anyway.

5-15

Sorry, you're just not ruthless enough. If you really want to make it as a Sly Golfer, you'll have to try much harder. Try snatching ice-creams from little children and reversing your car into old ladies on pedestrian crossings to toughen yourself up.

LESS THAN 5

There's no hope for you, I'm afraid. You're one of the good guys, doomed forever to a life of being shamelessly hustled on the golf course. You're one of that rarest of individuals, a good, honest, decent, upright and noble soul. You poor sucker.

CHAPTER FIFTEEN

EPILOGUE

So that's it—the great and noble sport of golf.

Don't forget, as a Sly Golfer, you still have much to learn. When you next watch the pros do battle on your screens, study them, and try to pick up more of the finer points of the game. As Seve Ballesteros kneels down to line up his putt, keep your eyes on Fuzzy Zoehler or Nick Faldo or Greg Norman or Tom Watson.

I swear you'll see them murmur: "Try and concentrate, Sev. Forget this one's for a quarter of a mill. Hell, it's only a game . . ."

THE TEN GOLDEN RULES OF SLY GOLF

1. THE END JUSTIFIES THE MEANS

2. STOP AT NOTHING

3. NEVER TRUST ANOTHER GOLFER

4. BE FRIENDLY, BE HELPFUL, BE CHEERFUL

5. THERE IS NO SUCH THING AS A HARMLESS JOKE

6. NEVER EVER BET ON YOUR OWN SKILL

7. FIND IT AND GRIND IT

8. DRIVE FOR SHOW, PUTT FOR DOUGH

9. NO ONE EVER GOT TO BE GREAT BY PLAYING IT STRAIGHT

10. WHEN YOU TAKE THE NOTES, REMEMBER TO GLOAT

Leslie Nielsen's Stupid Little Golf Book

Leslie Nielsen and Henry Beard

'I don't play golf to feel bad. I play bad golf, but I feel good'

LESLIE NIELSEN

To movie audiences worldwide, Leslie Nielsen is best known as the zany hero of the hilarious *Naked Gun* films. But to golf duffers around the globe, he has long been famous for a different role, as the World's Greatest Bad Golfer - the guru of bad golf.

Now, working with humourist and fellow hacker Henry Beard, Nielsen has drawn on a lifetime of brilliantly uninspired play to produce this unique collection of useless wisdom, spurious reminiscences and pointless tips, *The Stupid Little Golf Book*.

0-00-638683-0

The World's Best After-Dinner Jokes

Edward Phillips

Tall tales, naughty narratives and silly spoofs are all part of that hitherto unacknowledged literary genre, the after-dinner joke. Gathered together in this new collection are the *World's Best* specimens of this much-practised but rarely excelled at art form.

The old man was dying and he called his wife and family to his bedside. There were four sons – three fine big boys and a little one. He said to his wife in a weak voice, 'Don't lie to me now – I want to know the truth. The little one – is he really mine?'

'Oh yes, dear,' said his wife. 'He really is, I give you my word of honour.'

The old man smiled and slipped peacefully away. With a sigh of relief, the widow muttered, 'Thank God he didn't ask me about the other three!'

Containing the *crème de la crème* of the joke world, *The World's Best After-Dinner Jokes* is the perfect accompaniment to any meal.

ISBN 0 00 637960 5

More of the World's Best Drinking Jokes

Edward Phillips

You'll be well over the limit of humorous intake when you've finished this second hilarious cocktail of drinking jokes. A good measure of laughter is guaranteed!

Breaking with custom, a woman decided to have a Scotch and soda as a nightcap. After drinking it, she went upstairs to kiss her small son good night. After she had kissed him, he said, 'Mummy! You're wearing Daddy's perfume!'

Two friends were returning from a convivial evening at the local. 'Am I staggering at all?' asked one. 'If I am, the wife'll notice it and there'll be hell to pay. Hang on here a minute – I'll walk on ahead and you tell me if I'm walking straight.' He walked on a few steps and his mate said, 'You're all right – but the chap with you is staggering about all over the place.'

If you enjoy a tipple or two, you'll love this irresistible collection of *More of the World's Best Drinking Jokes!*

ISBN 0 00 637959 1

The World's Best Golf Jokes

Robert McCune

Whether you're a brilliant professional, an enthusiastic amateur or a golf widow, there's something for everyone to chuckle at in this hilarious collection of *The World's Best Golf Jokes*.

Side-splitting, saucy and entertaining, this book is a must for anyone who knows anyone who plays the ever-popular game of golf.

'I'd move heaven and earth to be able to break 100 on this course,' sighed the veteran.
'Try heaven,' advised the caddie. 'You've already moved most of the earth.'

'What's your golf score?' the country club interviewer asked the prospective new member.
'Well, not so good,' replied the golfer. 'It's 69.'
'Hey, that's not bad. In fact, it's very good.'
'Glad you think so. I'm hoping to do even better on the next hole,' the golfer confided.

0 00 638332 7

The World's Best Irish Jokes

Mr "O'S"

Paddy and Mick tread their way carefully among hapless parachutists, distraught submarines, dogs with flat noses, ingenuous priests, guileless colleens, fragmented bomb disposal experts and apocryphal men in pubs.

How many Irish jokes have you ever heard? And how many do you remember? Worry not – they're all here plus many more.

Mr "O'S" has tirelessly collected all those jokes that people have told him and his fellow countrymen. And he gratefully dedicates this volume to all those Irishmen who have courageously suffered the slings and arrows of outrageous slander and cheerfully donated their favourites to this libellous collection. Who else would have such wit and generosity? Who else would be so daft?

0 00 638409 9

The World's Best Scottish Jokes

Des MacHale

From kilts, haggis and whisky to Jock's legendary thriftiness, this hilarious collection of Scottish jokes is guaranteed to tickle the fancy of all those north – and south – of the border.

Heard the one about the Scottish obscene telephone caller? (He got caught because he kept trying to reverse the charges.)

What does a Scotsman think of Irish whiskey? It's useful stuff if you run short of water for diluting Scotch . . .

With Graham Thompson's wickedly appropriate cartoons, this is an irresistible addition to the World's Best Jokes series.

ISBN 0 00 638364 9

The World's Best Drinking Jokes

Ernest Forbes

The world's most popular joke series turns its attention to one of the world's most popular occupations... drinking.

The drunk rushed up the stairs to the fifth floor of a building and threw himself out of the window. A crowd gathered around him as he lay on the pavement. A policeman dashed to the spot and knelt beside the man, 'What happened?' 'Don't ask me,' said the drunk. 'I only got here myself.'

A drunk guest embraced a strange woman at a party. 'Excuse me, madam, but I thought you were my wife,' he mumbled apologetically as he realised his mistake.
'You're a fine husband to have,' said the irate lady, 'just look at you, you're a clumsy, drunken, disgusting brute.'
'Good heavens!' exclaimed the drunk. 'Not only do you look like my wife, you talk just like her, too.'

'Have you seen Anthony Hopkins as Titus Andronicus?'
'I don't know, how tight does Andronicus get?'

If you're fond of a drop – or know anyone who is – this is the book for you.

0 00 638242 8

Girl Chasing
How to Improve Your Game

Cathy Hopkins

With cartoons by Gray Jolliffe

For the first time in the history of sex, here is the definitive guide to understanding, charming – and winning – the ladies.

Cathy Hopkins, herself a girl and an expert on the complicated and often puzzling, female psyche, has produced a hilariously entertaining and comprehensive manual for all men who want to play the Girl Chasing Game, with lots of indispensible Game Plan information – how to meet them, flirt with them, interpret their body language, impress them, and even – perish the thought – how to cope with rejection!

ISBN 0 00 637940 0